Artisanal Slush
Ellora Sutton

For Hayley, who gave me my first
Animal Crossing *game.*

VERVE
POETRY PRESS
BIRMINGHAM

PUBLISHED BY VERVE POETRY PRESS
https://vervepoetrypress.com
mail@vervepoetrypress.com

FIRST PUBLISHED SEP 2023

Printed and bound in the UK
by Imprint Digital, Exeter

ISBN: 978-1-913917-43-2

CONTENTS

Hometown

There isn't even a McDonald's and the museum sells
postcards of the grave of a dismembered Victorian
schoolgirl. What is this place but a DVD in a book of
DVDs yellowing under my bed? That August we watched
rats perform their rusty knife-tricks by the chip shop's
open kitchen door and I thought only of my hunger, my
inability to drive. I am trying to talk to you about my heart.
How it is a salivating dog, an unattainable body, a
photocopy of a *LOST TORTOISE* flyer pinned to a
lamppost. How it reminds me of my mother. This stale
cough-candy town with its vandalised model village. Its
three churches, its sleepy terror. How every morning for
the past twenty-five years the same woman has stood by
the *Welcome* sign pointing her counterfeit speedgun, but still
this place drives it like it stole it to meet me, and my ribs
shatter to stardust every damn time.

*

      the cemetery trees wait
      like black dogs for the moon
      to say *heel*   to say

                    good dog

Archaeology Phrasebook

Bulb of percussion

When he explains, I am surprised. By flint's ability to scar. To be scarred. It seems such a human invention, an emotional one. This need to assign emotion. When really it's just hunger, all the way down.

Harris matrix

It's like being lost in IKEA. How it all gets very multi-burial very quickly and then you realise you're not even a feature, just a context *within* a feature. Like a dining room chair with a pleasing Scandinavian name mounted on a moveable wall. How, in any other context, it would be an art installation. How there would be a gift shop, selling postcards of *Dining Chair Without Table*. How I'd buy one and write a poem on the back of it, trying to justify all the money ever spent on ghost hunts.

Isotopes	And what could my teeth tell you? That I was never voted Miss Radiogenic, my isoscape is incomplete and my signal is terrible. Don't try to reach me, my tongue is always burnt. My mouth is an urn of deficiencies and impatience. Most of my problems would likely fix themselves if I just slowed down, really chewed my food, drank markedly less coffee.
Organic material	I get claustrophobic thinking about future archaeologists. How I have choked dead their pretty games of supposing. How obsolete I have rendered their tiny, delicate brushes. How without possibility, the cracked pottery of my algorithms.
Ritualistic	A cynical archaeologist tells me it doesn't mean anything. That it's slang for *we'll go mad not knowing*. I buy a cactus (again). I note in my diary when to water it. I plan to do better. To care not more, but better. I'm slowly filling my mouth with metal. Horses, not bullets. Sometimes, I think, there isn't a reason.

Wet-sifting Everything is destructive in its own
right, and isn't that kind? What I
want from the afterlife: this.
Watching dust float upwards, to
where we are. Water passing
through us, carrying away the seeds,
the charcoal. Leaving only light. So
much light we forget what living
was.

Self-Portrait as Formerly 'Gifted and Talented'

I am a grass stain of my former self, the direct-to-video sequel the original voice actors declined. Subliminal messages with their own Wikipedia page, my name a freezeframe of kicked-up dust huffed into the sky. No animator can please everyone but come *on*, my hair doesn't even look good when I cry. I'm twenty-six, I'm the mainstream-label corporate rock whore sell-out second album of my former self. I can't even play an instrument. I'm a payday loan of my former self. A spork, a microwave meal, I stop the timer twice to check I pierced the film. The films I watch are the same films I've always watched, old friends filling my mouth like steam from a pierced microwave dumpling, I know a good sauce for that. I'm the CV of my former self, an incomplete application for more, please. One of those big paper lanterns that gets tangled in telephone wires, spooks horses. I am a spooked horse of my former self, a bloodshot eye and thrown shoe. I've been wearing the same pair of boots for the past five years, I wake up in the middle of the night worrying about the day their black tongues finally split. Will there be feathers? Asbestos? Radioactive waste? I am a mushroom cloud of my former self. I'm a barely anthropomorphic mutt of my former selves. A terrifying howl. A loading symbol.

[*New password must be different from old password.*]

I think I might be Dennis Nedry

'Dogson! We've Dogson here! See, nobody cares!' – Dennis Nedry,
Jurassic Park (1993)

For I lack the leather of Dr Ian Malcolm when he says *I'm
always on the lookout for a future ex-Mrs Malcolm*

For I too would get over-excited in public about a fully-
functioning can of shaving cream with a hidden
compartment for transporting dinosaur embryos

For I hate my boss and would probably steal his dinosaur
embryos in return for $1.5 million and a free meal or, hell,
just for the meal

For I too play *Tetris* on company time

For I too will always choose myself without being able to
save myself

For I want someone to glimpse me through the foliage of
their final moments and for their final words before I eat
them to be *clever girl*

For my name is an anagram of bitterness

For I too wear hideous shirts, and was bullied in high
school

For I was voted Most Likely To Be Killed In The Pouring
Rain By A Venom-Spitting Technicolour Dinosaur

For I was voted Most Likely To Die Before The Movie
Really Gets Going Due To The Entirely Avoidable
Consequences Of My Own Actions

For my body was voted Most Likely To Never Be
Recovered

For the best I can hope for from the afterlife is to become
a meme

Self-Portrait as Facebook Ads

A Cento

teardrop print cotton pyjamas / madder red
orchard apple & dragon fruit
steeped in queer rage

try therapy online today

one theory is that he was the convicted killer
Lee Miller, Leonora Carrington

don't forget bad girls
          herbaceous flowers
there are only around 3,900 tigers left in the wild

                    Everyone Else Burns

Formal Apology to the Teacher Who Tried to Explain Dadaism to Me

I can see now Dadaism is relevant to everything
and probably always has been, e.g.
there is nothing more Dada than rhubarb
or the ruins of Pompeii. Miss,
if Putin nukes us all tomorrow, I want you to know
I went to Aldi last night without a bra,
their 99p rhubarb is amazing.
I saw the same kindly old gentleman twice –
the first time queuing up outside the pharmacy,
the second time in Aldi he said, 'hello, you!'
and I said, 'we must stop meeting like this!'
when what I meant was, 'you have a kind face,
I must tell you about the rhubarb'.
I'm paraphrasing. What I mean is
I learnt romance from Nigella Lawson
and the window of my Year Nine
maths classroom. Also partly
from life-sized oil paintings of horses.
By the time I realised I wanted to be Lisa Simpson
I was already older than Lisa Simpson. Miss,
I just want you to know
I don't remember your name,
you're probably an amalgamation
of older women from various pivotal moments in my life,
those moments that you don't realise are pivotal

until years later
when you find them
all warped and distorted like a crashed car in a forest
and you think, 'well, maybe Dadaism is relevant after all'.
Miss, if Putin nukes us all tomorrow
I'd do it all again, exactly the same,
apart from maybe
I'd summer in the Rhubarb Triangle,
the perfect setting for a time-travelling
screwball comedy such as this.

Tom Nook can't come to the phone right now. Please leave a message.

Hi, Tom. I know I haven't been around lately but I want you to know I haven't forgotten you. You were there for me, man. You gave me a place to stay when nothing made sense, broke it all down into small, manageable chunks when I couldn't even get dressed. You said 'what have you got' and when I said 'nothing' you said 'hey kid those cherries look nice' so I picked a load of cherries and they were nice and you said 'those cherries look nice' and bought them off me and suddenly I had money I had purpose and the cherries were really nice. You're a real Chandler Bing, Mr Nook. Y'know that episode where Chandler invents a game called Cups to trick Joey into taking money from him because he doesn't want Joey to feel bad about not being able to afford electricity or water. You're even better than Chandler Bing, Tom. I was no Joey Tribiani to you. I was nobody until you taught me how to make an axe, and then how to swing an axe. I was spiralling like a loading symbol. I was crying in the shower so you let me name your entire fucking island. Do you know what that does to a person, psychologically? How it can save a person? I'll never forget that. You were like a father to me. I know we don't talk so much nowadays but that's what I love about you – because I *do* love you, Tom – I know that you're always there. Anyway. Just thought I'd reach out.

Taste the Feeling

To wind down, I watch a two-hour documentary about the
late twentieth-century Cola Wars. I learn that Pepsi
changed everything when they asked random people on
the street to blind taste-test Pepsi and Coca-Cola and say
which they liked best. This was called *The Pepsi Challenge.*
The subjects almost always picked Pepsi, an expert
explains, because Pepsi has a sweeter first sip. I am making
dinner whilst I watch this. I picked it as a kind of self-
deprecating joke, thinking it would be a funny anecdote –
*oh yeah the other night I watched a two-hour documentary about
the late twentieth-century Cola Wars lol* – but I've found myself
so invested I don't care that the onions are burning. I'm more
invested in this than I was that stupid Viking documentary.
What does that say about me? I will likely never drink
mead from a drinking horn or set fire to a monastery with
all the monks still inside but I do mark every small,
colloquial victory with a glass bottle of full-sugar cola – by
which I mean, of course, Coca-Cola – and my favourite
poem is Frank O'Hara's 'Having a Coke with You' and you
just know he means the bright, love-red label of a glass
bottle of Coca-Cola for a longer-lasting, more sincere
sweetness. Frank O'Hara wants more than just a sip.

My computer thinks I'm gay

A zuihitsu after Placebo, co-written by InferKit AI

My computer is more myself than I am, it finishes my sentences but with better spelling. It remembers the plotlines of every 75k+ fanfic I've ever read, the definition of every act I've ever looked up on Urban Dictionary, how many times I've nearly bought a ukulele.

*

My iPad autocorrects Hiroshi Sugimoto's 'Cliffs of Moher' to 'Cliffs of Mother', and this is what they mean about robots replacing us. Saint Hildegard of Bingen linked the Latin *materia* (matter) to *mater* (mother), and toured Germany in 1158 as *The Sibyl of the Rhine*.

*

> My computer thinks I'm gay.
> And it's bringing all kinds of love to me.
>
> Every day, I go to the computer.
> The damned thing tries to give me a shag.
>
> Every day, I go to the computer.
> The damned thing tries to give me a shag.

But instead of shagging its spinning eyes I watch wrestling.

Instead of shagging its spinning eyes I watch wrestling.

Instead of shagging its spinning eyes I watch wrestling.

*

When I was filling out uni applications and ticked *prefer not to say* as my sexual orientation, did my computer roll its eyes and mutter *who does she think she's kidding?*

*

I only know about Saint Hildegard of Bingen because I opened Facebook at the right time, just as The Vagina Museum shared her illuminated illustration of the cosmos as a vulva, as shown to her by God.

*

And what does all of this mean for death?

*

I do my research. Hildegard wrote the earliest known description of the female orgasm *(vehement heat)* and the earliest known mention of cultivated lavender *(for oil)*. She adorned her nuns in gold and unbound their hair, wrote hymns to women called *Holy Medicine* and *Most Splendid of Gemstones*. She felt her visions physically. Her visions were, in all likelihood, migraines. Of all that's been lost, why hasn't this?

*

"Save the ones you wish to keep." – Microsoft Word Document Recovery

*

I'm a computer geek, so I could probably explain it to you, but I am still trying to figure it out.

The heavy rain isn't helping either.

*

Hildegard would have called this *divine inspiration*. Hinge calls it an algorithm.

Alternate Universes Only Really Work in Fanfiction

After 'Introduction to Quantum Physics' by Franny Choi

In this one   you run a coffee shop and nobody falls in love with you because you only express your true feelings through latte foam art.

In this one   you are in high school and nobody falls in love with you because, Jesus, do you remember yourself in high school?

In this one   you have a giant glittering pair of demonic wings and nobody falls in love with you because you don't realise you can fly until the penultimate chapter.

In this one   you are on the *Titanic* and nobody falls in love with you because you keep obsessing over the number of lifeboats and your final words before you hit the water are *I told you so.*

In this one   you get a roommate and nobody
falls in love with you because you
angry-cry whilst washing up
someone else's dirty spoons and
leave passive-aggressive post-it
notes on the fridge.

In this one   you work on yourself and nobody
falls in love with you but that's
okay, that's not the point, you had a
homemade pumpkin scone for
breakfast and tomorrow you'll
scatter the stale crumbs of your
leftovers, wait on the stoop for
birdsong –

Roses

I want to know more about roses.

I want to be given a rose, a yellow rose,

I want to be given a rose

by the kind of person who always carries secateurs

and they're giving it to me

just because they've read this poem about my wanting

to know more about roses. Their etymology.

I want it tucked into my hair. I have no interest in hair

apart from Kate Winslet's hair in *Titanic*

when she takes out that jewelled comb and shakes

her hair down over her shoulders like a French girl

or her almost-boyfriend's sketch of a French girl.

I suppose it symbolises her emancipation

or something. Maybe I should say

I don't care about roses apart from Rose in *Titanic*.

I've always felt that *Titanic* was a bit of a prologue.

Like, what does Rose do next? Where does she go?

I hope she mastered spitting not like a man but like herself.

I hope she spat herself dry.

I hope she spat into many mouths

and lived long enough to play *The Sims*,

to make herself and Jack on *The Sims* and watch him

teach their improbably gorgeous, pixelated children

how to walk. And at the very end
is Old Rose dead in Titanic Heaven
kissing Jack on that grand staircase
whilst her husband is up in Normal Heaven
watching like the rest of us, thinking
dude what the fuck? What the actual fuck?

As with most things, I blame My Chemical Romance

if you called me *pretty* right now

it would haunt every poem I will ever write

or have ever written

                thus is my limited understanding of

the fluid nature of time

based largely on *Doctor Who* reruns &

the ringing in my ears after the rock show

I've been waiting my whole life for

mouthing into the reverb like breathing

        I want you   *I want you*

to call me *pretty* whilst I puke Dark Fruits into a patch of
nettles in a sad layby

            && fuck

if you asked me right now

hey

    you   *okay*   *?*

I don't think I'd ever need to eat or write anything

        ever

          ever again

RIP Heather, you would have loved Taylor Swift

'A woman, known to us as 'Heather', was buried in Barrow 19. Analysis of her bones and teeth revealed she was around 20 years old and had moved to this area, but probably not from far away.' – Petersfield Museum and Art Gallery

We'd meet at a bar called Barrow 19. I'd think of every Hallmark movie I've ever seen and say *hey, you new in town?* Which would make you laugh, Heather, and I'd make a note in my phone saying *you laugh like a geophysical survey (so incomprehensible, so technicolour).* We'd laugh (together) at the debitage of boys flicking their lighters in the street. I'd laugh (harder) when you call them *composite tools*, make another note in my phone: *I can't even imagine how to bury you.*

We'd sit together every Sunday, sipping chai lattes, lots of whole milk, Heather, there would be plenty. I'd watch you work arrowheads for your Etsy side-hustle in our little fern-starred flat, so much natural light. They'd love us on TikTok, Heather, the culture shock, the queer beauty. *This is important,* you'd say to the camera, showing me the perfect angle to hit flint against marcasite to strike sparks but all I can do is ask my silly questions, trying (always) to make you laugh – *have you ever skinned a mammoth? Do you believe in ghosts? What does this bead mean? And this one? Which beads would you keep to remember me by?*

Honey, (you'd call me) *are you trying to die vicariously through me?*

I'd laugh, and then I'd stop laughing. Maybe it's true, Heather, maybe I am out here trying to write for you the kind of afterlife I want for myself. What's wrong with that?

You never asked me what I wanted from this poem. Ellora, you never even asked me my name.

Rad

After 'Portent' by Rachel Long

I feel like such a boy when I'm in love.

It makes me reckless,
makes me think I can do crazy shit
like down a gallon of milk in ten seconds,

like a kickflip
or halfcab broken fingers
even though I've never touched a skateboard in my life
& had to Google *cool skateboard tricks*
for the sake of this poem.

When I'm in love, I say things like
I would I so totally would & mean it
with my entire body & I love my body
because it enables me to love &

when I'm in love it's like I'm living
in the computer game *Tony Hawk's Pro-Skater 4*
where there is a glitch that means none of the keys do
what the in-game tutorial promised
& I play nonstop for hours & hours
kickflipping myself to death
like it's the entire point of the game

like I understand entirely
what I am doing.

New Horizons

Carrying only

- A lighthouse
- 9 oranges
- A wreath of blue roses
- 54 bags of sugar
- And a wetsuit

I board a seaplane called
Trainwreck French Toast
and fly to you

[loading...loading...]

Cottagecore AU

You enter through the kitchen and I am there
making good coffee slow in a metal pot on the stove
and I have never in my life burnt my tongue.

I have just taken scones out of the oven.
You ask *cream first or jam* and I say *yes*.
I tell you *Constable called clouds 'messengers'*
and you act like it's the first time.

The soil here is perfect for anything
and the light is just how I remember the light
in *Barbie Horse Adventures: Blue Ribbon Race*
on my old Game Boy Advance.

You are wearing a dress I made for you,
its deep pockets open-mouthed with flowers
you've picked for me on your way home
from chopping firewood, mending birdhouses.

And we live happily ever after,
like wishbones coughed up by the sun.

In a field on a clear night, I might say

I don't get what a belt is doing up there
in the stars, in the dark, come show me. Bruise me
into a gospel of consent, a manifesto on healing,
an art installation called *This is What I Want*
(Part I). Sit on the carpet outside your neoclassical
marble bathroom whilst I soak, reading out
the many five-star reviews of my performance
in the dual role of Courtney Love/John Keats
in my new one-woman musical *Your Teeth*
Are Only Unbroken Because I Choose It To Be So
in which the entire score was composed by an AI
asked to fantasise a lipstick factory after dark.

Prove to me that the best way
to increase the longevity of a cut rose
is to cut it again and cauterise the stem.
Prove that my middle name is Rose,
past tense of rise, raze me.
Tell me I am one hot zombie, almost hot enough
to be declared legally alive, clinically a miracle.

What do I have to offer you?

>   Permission
>   to call me *pretty* between dreams,
>   to witness my wild dreaming.

NOTES & ACKNOWLEDGEMENTS

'Archaeology Phrasebook' and 'RIP Heather, you would have loved Taylor Swift' were written as part of a residency at Petersfield Museum and Art Gallery.

'Self-Portrait as Facebook Ads'. Sources are Facebook adverts from the following pages: TOAST, Candy Kittens, Reading Rep Theatre, Better-Help, History Hit, Design Museum, Holybourne Theatre, Wild, WWF UK, All 4.

'Tom Nook can't come to the phone right now. Please leave a message.' Tom Nook is the mentor character in the videogame series *Animal Crossing*. He is a racoon; he is your landlord. *Animal Crossing: New Horizons* was released at the start of the first UK coronavirus lockdown.

"My computer thinks I'm gay" is the opening line of 'Too Many Friends' by Placebo. The indented sections were by generated by feeding this line to the InferKit AI demo online. Sources on Saint Hildegard of Bingen: *V* by Florence Schechter; *Femina* by Janina Ramirez; *The Other Side* by Jennifer Higgie; *The Story of Flowers* by Noel Kingsbury.

'Roses' was first published by *Berlin Lit.*

'As with most things, I blame My Chemical Romance' was first published by *Popshot.*

'New Horizons' is set in the world of *Animal Crossing: New Horizons*. "Trainwreck French Toast" is a seaplane name generated randomly by the game.

'Cottagecore AU'. 'AU' is fanfiction shorthand for 'Alternate Universe'.

This pamphlet started life when I was on a week-long Arvon at Home course taught by Cynthia Miller and Stephen Sexton. Thank you for putting the play back into my poetry, and making me realise the generative power of enjoying things.

Thank you to Petersfield Museum and Art Gallery for my wonderfully generative experience as their Poet-in-Residence. Special thanks to Ryan, Jeremy, and Molly. Thank you to Arts Council England for supporting the residency.

Endless gratitude to Isabelle Baafi for her clear and generous editorial eye, for pushing me to make these poems the best versions of themselves. These pages are far richer for your input.

Thank you, as ever, to my family and my teachers.

ABOUT THE AUTHOR

Ellora Sutton, she/her, is a poet and museum person based in Hampshire. Her work has been published or is forthcoming in *bath magg*, *The Poetry Review*, *Popshot*, *The North*, *Oxford Poetry*, and others. She reviews poetry for *Mslexia*, and is poet-in-residence at Petersfield Museum and Art Gallery, a position she has previously held at Jane Austen's House. Her debut pamphlet, *antonyms for burial*, Fourteen Poems, 2022) was the Poetry Book Society Spring 2023 Pamphlet Choice.

She tweets @ellora_sutton, or you can find her at ellorasutton.com.

ABOUT VERVE POETRY PRESS

Verve Poetry Press is an award-winning press that focussed initially on meeting a local need in Birmingham - a need for the vibrant poetry scene here in Brum to find a way to present itself to the poetry world via publication. Co-founded by Stuart Bartholomew and Amerah Saleh, it now publishes poets from all corners of the UK and beyond - poets that speak to the city's varied and energetic qualities and will contribute to its many poetic stories.

Added to this is a colourful pamphlet series, many featuring poets who have performed at our sister festival - and a poetry show series which captures the magic of longer poetry performance pieces by festival alumni such as Polarbear, Matt Abbott and Imogen Stirling.

The press has been voted Most Innovative Publisher at the Saboteur Awards, and has won the Publisher's Award for Poetry Pamphlets at the Michael Marks Awards.

Like the festival, we strive to think about poetry in inclusive ways and embrace the multiplicity of approaches towards this glorious art.

https://vervepoetrypress.com
@VervePoetryPres
mail@vervepoetrypress.com